W9-DBL-040

DEFILED TREASURE

STAYCE L. BYNUM

Love Clones Publishing
www.lcpublishing.net

Copyright © 2014 by Stayce Bynum. All rights reserved. This book or any portion thereof may not be reproduced or used in any manner whatsoever without the express written permission of the publisher except for the use of brief quotations in a book review.

Printed in the United States of America

First Printing, 2014

ISBN: 978-0692208250

Love Clones Publishing

332 S Michigan Ave – Ste 1032 #N455
Chicago, IL 60604
www.lcpublishing.net

DEDICATION

This book is dedicated to my greatest fan, my Number One cheerleader and the only one who has supported me, no matter what I endeavored upon. I dedicate this to My Mother, Ms. Annye Bynum, for without you I would not be alive. Our journey together has not always been a picture perfect one, but it has taught me everything I needed to bring this project to life. Thank you. You are a strong example of what it means to live life to the fullest.

To my Daddy, Mr. Earnest Burston, forever I will remain a Daddy's Girl. You spoiled me to the core, no one will take your place. I hope you are proud of me. To my Godmother Dr. Esther B. Philips, you taught me who God was at an early age and because of that, I am who I am today. I hope you both are proud of me as you look down from Heaven. To the rest of my family, you are special to me and I hope my love for you is shown within these pages.

I love you!

SPECIAL THANK YOU!

Thank you to my Lord and Savior Jesus Christ for without him I am absolutely nothing. He saw something in me and held my hand until I was able to see it, too. I am grateful for his amazing grace in allowing me to tell my story and bring glory to his name.

A special thank you to my Pastor, Bishop Oscar E. Brown and my First Lady Jacqueline D. Brown for your constant love, prayers and support as I walked this journey. Your spiritual leadership has meant so much to me that no words can really express my heart.

To the three most precious Sista-girls a woman could ever ask for – you cried with me and listened to me when I called late at night or early in the morning to seek your council. Thank you for pulling me through some rough patches and seeing me through to victory.

FOREWORD

My wife, Lady Jacqueline D. Brown, introduced me to the author of this work over 25 years ago. I would have called her anything but a "Defiled Treasure." She was so well packaged that neither I, nor anyone around her could tell that she was bound by generational strongholds or operating with dysfunctions.

After she gave her life to The Lord, I watched The Lord strip the facade off of her and rebuild her from the inside out. As her Pastor, I saw her weather through personal and public storms. At the time of her struggles, she did not think it was God bringing her to the revelation that she was a "Defiled Treasure."

Now, she can speak with great authority that God brought her out of bondage and she understands that her responsibility is to rescue others who have been born or brought into a defiled state. As you read her story, please understand that this author has lived each page of this book. As I have watched her go from a Defiled Treasure to a Developed Treasure, know that your life will also be transformed as you face your own demons. It is my prayer that as Stayce L. Bynum lays out her life to help empower you, God will continue to keep her as a vessel and treasure of honor.

Thank you, Stayce, for being brave enough to tell your story, which is not just your testimony but many of us share the same story. Having this treasure in earthen vessels has turned out to be the pathway to reaching others.

Bishop Oscar E. Brown
Senior Pastor, First Mt. Olive Freewill Baptist Church

INTRODUCTION

"But we have this treasure in earthen vessels, that the excellency of the power may be of God and not of us"
II Corinthians 4:7

Imagine a treasure chest of jewels that sparkle with all of the brilliance of a million stars. Its luminance makes it hard for you to even look at everything all at once. There is so much to see and your anxiety builds just at the thought of what else is inside. Yes, you notice some nice pieces that might be worthy of keeping safe, but remain passive. You realize what you have could be of some value one day, but you still may not fully understand the magnitude of the gift. As days and years go by, admirers stop by to see what all of the hoopla is about. They were attracted by the outward shine, but remained ignorant of the value. You couldn't tell them just how precious this treasure was because you really didn't know, yourself. Time passes and passersby have handled your jewels with dirty hands. Some of the hands even tried to remove a few pieces of your treasure. Over time, what once had luster and brilliance began to fade and what was initially so very special doesn't seem so special anymore. On occasion, you stop and try to dust them off in hopes of once again finding the shine your treasure once had until one day all of a sudden the dullness has become a grimy film. You notice that your treasure has become defiled. Touched and mishandled by the wrong hands and ignored, and just plain old neglect has resulted in a defiled treasure.

This story was my story and may even be your story. God

1

made each of us with a treasure buried inside. He wants to show us off to the world, but sometimes we are unaware of our value or over time forget about our significance or worth and allow influences, without and within, to tarnish us. So much so that eventually our treasures become unrecognizable – to ourselves and others. *Defiled Treasure* tells of my journey from low self-esteem, sexual sin and rejection, all as a result of generational strongholds. I allowed others to mishandle me and my treasures and had to work my way back to reclaiming the treasure chest full of beautiful and vibrant jewels. Defiled Treasure is authentic and will mirror your struggle in many ways. As we search for ways to find relief from the pain of our past, we must first stop and contemplate why the pain is there in the first place. Much of our pain stems from injuries from long ago that we simply refuse to acknowledge and therefore we go throughout our lives bearing the stench of past hurt and misery. But, there is one root cause that many of us could quite possibly be bearing the fruit of, and that is fruit from past generations.

MOVING DAY

Bound beneath the clutter of debris that stripped my spirit
Overwhelmed by what was packed away and
smothered by neglect
Wondering which way to flow, should I die or should
I live?
With all that's been stolen from me, is anything
left to give?
Searching for the right place like a dancer finds her groove
Afraid of what I knew all along, the spirit prompting me
to move
Moving from the comfort zone to the place of
accountability
Stepping out on faith; with no strings attached, new found
integrity
Opening locked shudders that break forth glorious new
light
Anticipating the early dawn that births a brand new day
Rearranging all of the precious things and inviting
love to stay
Making plans, awaiting destiny on this my Moving Day

Happy Valentine's Day, Stayce! It's Valentine's Day 2014, the eve of my forty-sixth birthday, and I am contemplating my current situation: single with no prospects in sight. It's another year of posting the Singles' Awareness Day pictures on Facebook and another year of wondering if this will be the last one… alone. Don't get me wrong, this year is quite different. Okay, I'll admit, it would be nice to go on a date, but I'm okay if it doesn't happen. I am in another place in my life now and the reality of my situation doesn't haunt me like before. It has occurred to me that once I became an adult, let's say from the age of twenty-five until now, I had never experienced a meaningful relationship in which I was free to receive the love and respect that I truly deserved. The cycle and pattern of relationships that I always found myself in never afforded me the opportunity to be seen in public or for any amount of quality time in private, for that matter. My self-esteem lacked the wherewithal to alert me of the deficiency of Vitamin "ME", so I took what I could get at the time. If any of this sounds familiar don't fret; all is not lost and you are not doomed to a life of low self-esteem or always being placed on the damaged goods shelf.

Since this was my life for so long, it begged the question "Why?" Why had my life turned out the way it did? Why was I always finding myself in the same situation or some version of the same situation? Why, when everything on the outside seemed so put together, was my real, intimate, private life so jacked-up? After years of searching and crying out to God, He finally allowed me to become privy to the root cause. I've learned never to take things at face value; there is always something deep beneath the surface which eventually manifests itself on the outside. When I acknowledged the problem, I knew it was time to move. Move from my insecurities and from shame to freedom, victory, self-worth and power. So, what did God show me? Why had I ended up in the same dysfunction with regards to my relationships? Read on. What was revealed to me certainly was not something I would have imagined in a million years. My dysfunction, and perhaps yours, began from my family tree. Destructive family habits, or what are sometimes described as generational strongholds, are passed down from one generation to the next and if not broken will create a cycle of dysfunction for years to come. A generational stronghold is not a new concept emerging over the last few years, but they have existed since the beginning of time and will continue until time is no more. So the questions loom, "Are we doomed to live with them forever?" Not necessarily. "Do we, ourselves, have a way out?" Most certainly! There is deliverance waiting for the one who will surrender to the process of breaking free and moving beyond the comfort zone.

However, your freedom will come at a cost. Surely you didn't think you could find deliverance without being crushed or fragmented, did you? Strongholds are not easily broken, especially when you have not identified or acknowledged them. The topic of generational strongholds is not typically a dinnertime conversation nor is it one that is easily broached, for its name alone suggests something or someone was to blame. This book is not to show you how to point the finger at anyone, or pass judgment; it is a tool of deliverance and freedom. It is my goal to bring my family members, and you my sisters and brothers out of bondage that you have not had the courage to confront until now. Normally, when we ignore something or fail to feed it, it dies; not in the case of a generational stronghold. Our lack of attention to it is precisely how the generational stronghold gets its strength and lingers within families for generations upon generations. Ignorance, or lack of knowledge, will give life to the generational stronghold. So, the million dollar questions are "How do we know when/if there is a stronghold in our lives?" or "How do we break these chains that have kept our families in bondage for so many years?" It will take downright raw honesty.

It will also require a spiritual intuition that is in tune to certain behaviors within our own lives, and a prayerful curiosity that will drive us to look deeper into the lives of family members around us. Sometimes strongholds are uncovered as the result of a casual conversation, as was in my case, between family members that triggers a red flag to delve deeper beyond the surface and to take note of certain habits and behaviors. Whatever the case may be, these strongholds must be identified, acknowledged and demolished if you are to get to your freedom. It's the courageous soul who understands that if they step up to the plate and accept the responsibility of destroying the stronghold they are in for a fight. This is why having spiritual insight and tenacity is essential. John 10:10 says that "the enemy comes to steal, kill and to destroy…" You will not simply go to the front lines and declare victory overnight, on the contrary, your tour of duty will be met with opposition, denial, and frustration – but you will not be defeated, if you don't quit. You are the ultimate victor if you stay in the fight and allow the Holy Spirit to be your Commander in Chief. I wish to take you on my journey of self-discovery of the generational stronghold that manifested within my family tree and in my life. A generational stronghold is not as easily identified as you might think. It is not something that manifests itself so overtly that it stares you in the face. On the contrary, it manifests as subtly as everyday life. Behaviors and addictions such as jealousy, alcoholism, drug abuse, attitudes, or sexual sin are but a few of the habits that might be generational strongholds within families. We sometimes think those behaviors start with us as the result of our response to an event in our lives, so we don't even stop to think if someone else in our family has had the same issue. In other cases, unfortunately, we do initiate the stronghold and those who come after us will experience the effects. Generational strongholds have arrested the development of greatness within our lives and in the lives of our family members. Down through the ages, they have destroyed mother/daughter, father/son, siblings and husband/wife relationships. I have found that I am not exempt, and neither are you. It has shown up in my life and I have been given a charge to destroy its presence and operation and to save the generation after me. In recent years, I have spoken to men and women who, unbeknownst to them, are dealing with a generational stronghold. They are being held hostage by the hurt from their past and somewhere inside longing to break free. My prayer is that you will use my story to help you gain insight and freedom from the chains that were meant to hold you from your destiny in God. I pray that this book will encourage you to look deeper into your past and present in order to save your future. I hope you are encouraged by my story of triumph and provoked to gain your own victory.

So this Valentine's Day is not a sad day at all. I am confident in myself and proud as punch that although I'm not spending it with anyone, I'm no longer compromising my integrity for the sake of artificial affection. Moving Day feels so good!

DEAR SISTER

The longer I live, the more I see the anguish and hurt of women everywhere. Pain that has resulted from abuse and molestation. The misfortune that so many have endured makes me shudder. After hearing so many stories of the pain, humiliation and, low self-worth, I walk around looking into the eyes of my sisters wondering to myself, "Has she been abused?" "Has she, too, been molested as a child?" I can see your pain in the way you dress- so seductively when a simple tee-shirt and pair of jeans would do. I can hear it in your words – condescending and angry tones. I was there. I can see it on your face – constantly walking around with an attitude of indifference and apathy. Where is your smile? I see you all made-up, impeccably dressed, and successful in your careers and home lives, all wearing a façade because you have been scarred in some way long ago. How do I know? I've been there and everyday I'm fighting to stay free from ever returning to that place of pain and isolation.

I have never been the victim of molestation, but I have been a victim of abuse; abuse of my emotions, my body, my trust and my loyalty. Any way you slice it, abuse is abuse. Yours may not look like mine; and mine is certainly different than yours. Nevertheless, something or someone took the right and mishandled us, or at some point in our lives, we gave permission.

This offense oftentimes transforms women from delicate, feminine images of God's beauty to angry, hardened, resentful females who were never created to live that way.

I have lived the story of most women scorned and left

with low self-esteem as my companion. I now live the life of freedom from the strongholds that once tried to issue me a life sentence with no possibility of parole. Through numerous struggles and faith failures, God still had a plan for my life. I finally realized that everything I had to experience was for you, my Dear Sister. Within these next chapters, you will see yourself as I become the mirror with which you see the root of your strongholds, your insecurities and low self-esteem.

Like most of you, my sisters, I've experienced being in a long-term relationship, then having the relationship end. I've experienced low self-esteem, and the feeling that no one else would ever be attracted to me. I've experienced a mild recovery of self-esteem or what I thought was self-esteem only to fall into a relationship to fill my lonely nights. But now as I write, my words take on a different tone, one that has matured over the ten plus years it has taken to see this work published. I am experiencing a life of waiting on the Lord and posturing myself to do whatever He asks. I am no longer afraid to put any and all unhealthy relationships away. Initially, upon writing this book, the underlying tone was to write how I was surviving and still waiting on the Lord to send me a mate. Instead, my view has changed dramatically to one that focuses on discovering the life that God has purposed for me. Somewhere in my divine purpose, I have learned to concentrate my energy on activating my singleness for God, listening to his voice and preparing for the anointing God has especially for me.

In retrospect, looking at the choices I have made as a

woman, I can say most assuredly that I was operating out of desperation. Desperation can cause you to do foolish things. Desperation can cause you to devalue yourself and lose sight of just how much you are worth. Desperation, among other things, can defile the treasure God has placed inside of you. Desperation is a trick of the enemy. Desperation for a lousy meal caused Esau to lose his birthright. It distorts our vision and rationale so that even the bitter things taste sweet. "The full soul loatheth an honeycomb; but to the hungry soul every bitter thing is sweet." ~Proverbs 27:7

The Lord is using me and my experiences to help someone run from destruction that may take the form of generational strongholds, abusive relationships or behavior. Run from anything that is robbing you of your joy and your service to the Lord and discover the jewel, or better yet – the treasure that you are inside.

I once heard a well-respected Bishop say, "it's time to master that which has mastered me." Isn't that what the Lord wants us to do?

Ladies, in order for us to receive the blessings that are stored up for us and to operate as women of virtue we must be determined to lay aside every weight (sexual immorality, unhealthy relationships, insecurity, generational strongholds and attitudes) that so easily causes us to stumble into traps. These things prevent us from becoming a beautiful fragrance in God's nostrils. They prevent us from becoming better wives to our spouses and better friends to those around us.

How will you begin to prepare for the assignment God has placed over your life? Have you looked back at the events in your life that seemed unfair, that seemed to overwhelm your very being? Have you dismissed them as simply unfortunate periods of life that came and went? Don't underestimate the value of your experiences, they are the catalysts and stepping stones into your destiny. As you read some of my most intimate moments that, at times, will seem like a soap opera you will ask yourself, "Can she be that stupid?" My friends, in the end you will see how God used every single event in my life to bring me to this appointed season. At times I tried to end the season of preparation early, only to be pushed back and pruned some more. But thanks be to God who gives us the victory, He's brought me to the place He has prepared for me. If you are fighting within yourself because of low self-esteem or a generational stronghold or anything else trying to keep you bound, know that those walls can and will come down. Take it from me.

GENESIS OF A STRONGHOLD

Everyone has events in their lives that serve as turning points. Whether we recognize them or not at the time, they shape the decisions we make in the future. Pardon me as I park here to preface the remainder of this book by telling you when I experienced my turning point and I entered into the realm of my stronghold. I'm sure if I could go back in time and stand outside of myself, I would see a door in the spirit in which I entered that started my journey. As I write, I think about my very first relationship in which I spent 15 years of my life. My whole world revolved around this relationship so much so that I almost didn't breathe unless I asked him first. I experienced every 'first' in this relationship. I lost total control and I lost the essence of who I was to become. This relationship was marked by infidelity, but I didn't care - I loved him. I would be in denial of his actions and conclude that it must have been something I was lacking. For instance, once after finding him cheating on me, he made me feel so bad I sent him a bouquet of balloons the next day. WHO DOES THAT?

Somehow the enemy had me tricked into believing that this man needed me for something. I lost who I was and morphed into anything he wanted me to be. He needed me. He needed my car, my cooking and I just knew he needed my body. Everyone warned me about placing all of my proverbial eggs in one basket, but I didn't listen. My pastor and his wife tried to warn me. Each time I called them with the drama they listened and kept praying. In my mind, they

13

didn't understand. What did they know, besides, they were married and already had the life of which I had always dreamed. As time and experience would tell, they loved and cared very much for me.

I stayed in this relationship for eight years after graduating high school and we even had plans to marry. I should have known something was wrong when he couldn't even tell his mother that we were engaged. Way to go for the secret engagement! I ignored the subtle signs of disaster. Well, he cheated some more and I forgave some more. Until one day, five months before our wedding (after almost everything was paid for), in counseling he came to me and said he really wasn't ready to go through with the wedding. Now, that was probably the only time he ever told the truth.

After that, my world ended. I wanted to stop breathing. I was left alone. However in reality, I was not alone; God had other plans. When we find ourselves operating in God's permissive will, He will allow things to happen to get our attention. Some do not believe in God's permissive will, and that's okay, these are my thoughts. He will allow us to move ahead with our plans until he decides enough is enough, however it is still up to us to make the choice to follow God or to follow our will. Abraham and Sarah operated out of God's permissive will, how do you think they got Ishmael? We've all got an Ishmael...or a few. The question is will we allow Ishmael to teach us the lesson, or constantly complain of his existence? Use that joker to crush the enemy's head! Something had to break and it was me. This was just the beginning of preparation to do God's will for my life.

Sometimes God will allow chaos to enter our lives in order to get us to move. For some, we only get on our knees when we are in trouble. I know because that is how I used to operate. Initially, I resisted God's instructions to walk away and be free. I was not mature enough to see things in the spirit, so operating out of flesh, I misjudged any attention from my ex in the months, even years to follow as a sign from God that our relationship would be reconciled.

Isn't it funny how our flesh can manipulate our thinking and our ability to receive what is healthy for our lives? All of my prayers for 2 ½ years were that the Lord would work on my ex and bring him back to me. I prayed for any sign in any direction that pointed to reconciliation. I remember praying that if I had any type of communication from him after I finished praying on any particular day it would mean he was coming to his senses. It actually happened on a few occasions. I was excited, silly me. I was confusing spiritual things with normal, everyday occurrences that just happened with life. I prayed that I'd look better to him, perhaps, if I dressed a certain way, or acted a certain way and he would want to come back and be with me. I even went so far as to cut my hair because I got wind that he liked short hair. Who was I? Unknown to me, God was working on me and what I believed were two and a half years wasted, were not wasted at all. Slowly my prayers began to turn to asking the Lord to take the desire away from me because the fact remained he had other women all over the place. I couldn't forget my first love. Who can? I was too needy and that will either drive people from you or open the door for them to take advantage of you. From this first relationship I learned to never allow another person to have that much control over me. I continued to pray for signs of release…

I thought I would know the day and the hour God would deliver me. God, just being God, did it without even consulting me. One day I just woke up and the thoughts were few and far between. The constant nightmare I had when we were together was one that spoke volumes and told me everything I needed to know. I ignored it, though. In the nightmare I would constantly catch him with other women and I would try to hurt him physically. I would fight and claw at him but he just would not go away. Another recurring dream was one where I would always find myself being held captive. I would be tied up or kidnapped and taken away. My attackers would always try to hurt me or even kill me. They threw knives, shot me in the head, you name it. Amazingly enough I was never harmed or killed. Could you imagine being afraid to go to sleep at night for fear of your dreams? To me, those dreams meant the bondage, in which, the enemy was trying to keep attached to me. It represented the danger and in a strange way the reassurance of my protection. Isaiah 54:17 states "no weapon formed against me shall prosper…" It didn't say the weapon wouldn't be formed, it just wouldn't prosper. Never dismiss the signs that the Holy Spirit will bring to you in order to protect you.

Another sign of freedom was that the nightmare stopped. I hadn't noticed the connection before. One day I just realized that I didn't hurt anymore. I slept soundly. I had no one in my life hurting me. That felt good. I still had a long way to go though, because although he wasn't hurting me, I was still hurting myself. My behavior following this relationship would reveal this fact. I went through depression of not having someone in my life. I thought my ex was the only one on planet earth that would ever want me. The devil is a liar! I tried the single sisters groups, but after a while that didn't satisfy me. I was not ready to face me and see who I really was. My sisters, is any of this resonating with you, yet? However it did plant the seed in realizing I needed to develop a healthy self-esteem and self-love that no one else could ever give to me. Sister, please hear me, you are worth so much more than you actually realize. Our value is not predicated on how much a man loves us or even if we have the ability to keep that man in our lives. The Word of God tells us in Psalm 139 that we are "fearfully and wonderfully made". No one knows better than I do about being lonely and the behavior that spirit manifests. God, through the work of the Holy Spirit, is able to keep you, if you allow Him. It feels much better having a faithful God hold you than having someone or something robbing you of your worth.

I also know what it feels like having someone in your space and still feeling alone. It is a learning process to become content in your state. Be committed to the process. When we focus on the tasks the Lord has for us as women – married or single, we can serve the Lord without distraction.

I know you are probably saying to yourself, "yeah, all of those words sound good, but how do I put them into action?" I'm glad you asked…come and discover how I finally gave it all to the Lord and watched Him reveal the root of my dysfunction which manifested in the form of a generational stronghold and allowed Him to fill the empty spaces inside of me.

ANATOMY OF A STRONGHOLD

On the day we are born, we make our entrance into what we now know as our lives. After nine months of gestation, labor and much pain, we strategically made our way through the birth canal and were ready to face the world in all of our glory. We did not get to pick the families we were born into, we just showed up. And because we did not get to pick, we were subject to the idiosyncrasies and flaws which were passed down from generation to generation. Within our family structure lie certain behaviors that sometimes make their way into the behavior of the other family members. Good or bad, what we grow up witnessing as children plays a part in defining our lives as adults.

For example, some families possess a generational blessing of entrepreneurship or wealth, whereby family members have a natural inclination to build business, good stewardship and generational wealth, whereas, families with generational strongholds exhibit just the opposite and manifest destructive patterns of poverty or lack, within family members. Habits and traits that we may feel are inconsequential can very well turn out to be the very self-destructing patterns that the enemy will use to destroy our future and our destiny and that of our families. God has a plan for each of us and that plan is a good one. The word of God says in a very familiar passage of scripture, "I know the thoughts that I think towards you, saith the Lord, thoughts of peace, and not of evil, to give you an expected end." Jer. 29:11 KJV The enemy also knows that God has a plan and he has seen the trailer into your future and devised a way to do all he can to abort it. The bible says "for we are his (God's) workmanship, created in Christ Jesus unto good works, which God had before ordained that we should walk in them." Ephesians 2:10 (KJV). The enemy does not want us to walk in what God has created for us.

How does the enemy try to cancel our plans? He does so by subtle tactics which are meant to throw us off course, using generational strongholds as one of his weapons of mass destruction. It is important to understand the definition and nature of what we have come to know as a generational stronghold. Generational strongholds are "habits and tendencies handed down within families which manifest throughout periods of a person's lifetime, until they are broken." If we take a good look at our ancestors and immediate family members, more than likely we would be able to identify some type of behavior, or tendency that has manifested as a family trait. I will reiterate here what I mentioned in a previous chapter that this is not meant for you to go looking for a stronghold so you can place blame or cause someone to feel ashamed or hurt, this information is meant to expose the enemy for who he is and cancel his diabolical plan in our lives. Let me say now that I come against the spirit of accusation and release the spirit of wisdom, In Jesus' Name! Understandably, some will not comprehend this notion, so please know when and if you can share and shed light on this topic in your family.

Strongholds may come in the form of alcohol or drug abuse, sexual sin, divorce or poverty. Strongholds could also manifest as a spirit of jealousy, spirit of rejection and a whole host of other issues. For example, a poverty stronghold would manifest itself through a parent on welfare and subsequently their children on welfare and their children's children on welfare, and so the cycle would continue. The same can hold true for divorce. Let's say your parents are divorced, your grandparents were divorced, and now you're fighting to keep your marriage together. That could very well be a generational stronghold that needs to be broken. Certainly, those were just elementary examples, but you get the picture. God feels very strongly about families and talks a lot about generations in His word. Exodus 34:6-7 reads, *And he passed in front of Moses, proclaiming, "The Lord, the Lord, the compassionate and gracious God, slow to anger, abounding in love and faithfulness, maintaining love to thousands, and forgiving wickedness, rebellion and sin. Yet he does not leave the guilty unpunished; he punishes the children and their children for the sin of the parents to the third and fourth generation."*

The topic of generational strongholds is not one often discussed among families because these habits or traits are simply dismissed as "something we do" or "that's just how the women are in this family". These generational strongholds do not only exist among the people of God, they exist within humanity at-large. It's just that the world doesn't label their dysfunction as a stronghold. As long as these issues go on without being identified and addressed, the stronger the chains and the harder they will be to break once God reveals that the cycle stops with you.

Generational strongholds are not new; they didn't just start showing up in families over the last few centuries, they existed long ago and were present among our most prominent of biblical heroes. In the book of Genesis we see a stronghold of deceit and lack of integrity that started with Abraham when he lied to Abimelech by saying that Sarah was his sister instead of his wife. His lie was the result of trying to control the outcome of a situation, which in turn, placed someone else at risk. Later on in Genesis, we see Isaac, Abraham's son, repeating the same pattern of deceit by lying and saying that Rebekah was his sister instead of his wife. It doesn't stop there. Then we see Jacob, Isaac's son and grandson to Abraham, who tricked his brother, Esau out of his birthright and Rebekah, Jacob's own mother who convinces him to deceive his father Isaac into giving him the blessing. Jacob's name even means "trickster" or "surplantor".

Even David, the man after God's own heart had a stronghold to deal with that manifested through his children. But just as God was able to restore and use them, He can do the same for us if we find ourselves dealing with a generational stronghold.

Perhaps you are thinking about some behaviors in your own life and family right now. You would not be alone. Acknowledging the existence of generational strongholds is the first step to deliverance. When you and I refuse to identify and confront what has been in our lives for years and present in our relatives before us, we risk forfeiting a life of abundance and victory the way God intended. We hear of generational curses and strongholds within the church and shy away from the topic because we do not want to believe that we are "cursed". Certainly I am not suggesting that you go to your family and say, "did you know that this family was cursed?!" What will happen is they will look at you like you're crazy! We must use wisdom when confronting this issue; it is vitally important. When we talk about anything generational, it means that we must go back to those that came before us to carefully glean information. It could mean a subtle conversation about what you've taken notice of within your own life or the lives of certain members of the family. Typically, our fore parents don't open up about certain things in their past, perhaps due to cultural norms, so therefore we must also be prayerful that the Holy Spirit will also reveal things to us.

When trying to identify a stronghold, you can perform an exercise as simple as drawing a quick family tree and see if you can connect your struggle with another family member or members. Is there some behavior in your life that you've found yourself asking why you do what you do? Have you stopped to ask, "Did mom or dad do this?" Do you find yourself drinking excessively like some other family members? Have you found yourself only ending up in destructive relationships that rob you of your self-worth? These struggles and strongholds were designed to keep you in bondage and the issue perpetuated deep within your bloodline.

But you need to remember that as a child of God, you have a new bloodline and there are no strongholds in God, for He came to set the captive free. "He has sent me to bind up the brokenhearted, to proclaim freedom for the captives and release from darkness for the prisoners." Isaiah 61:1 (KJV)

MY STRONGHOLD REVEALED

An "aha!" moment is that point in time or experience when you have a certain sudden insight or realization. It's that moment when you finally get to the bottom of an issue, or the moment you feel you finally got that lesson God had been trying to teach. It is at that moment that you feel you are ready to move on with a plan of action. That moment for me came back in my mid to late twenties, but I did not execute my plan of action until years later. My "aha!" moment was a revelation of sorts. It explained why I allowed myself to be mishandled by the men in my life. Revelation comes in layers, a piece at a time, because we are not always able to handle the truth all at once. We need time to process and be honest with ourselves and what was just exposed about our lives. For me, that moment took me back to years prior in my first relationship and everything I had experienced. My "aha" moment caused me to ask some questions once I was able to regroup. Are we the sole determining agent of our actions, habits and tendencies? Are some of our character traits the result of something from our past that we simply do not know about? How much control do we *really* have?

It is not the norm to dissect every habit that we have in search of a genesis on which to attach, but at some point in our lives, it's worth a journey to our past to save our future. For some, it may not even be a habit it could be those things we attract to our lives. We sometimes attract the wrong types of individuals and spirits to our space and we just don't know why. If we are not spiritually in tune, we won't even have the wherewithal to even stop and ask ourselves the question. In my case it was just that. After the failure of my very first relationship, I was left broken and numb to all sensibility. As a result, I went after who I wanted in search of proving a point to myself and the one who initially hurt me. When we face rejection, we go after a remedy that will show us any type of attention to validate our little false sense of self. In the case of a relationship, we think to ourselves, "Well, if they don't want me, I'll find someone who will." We do this at the expense of our self-worth. My low self-esteem was birthed out of the rejection I felt from my failed relationship. When you are hurting, you will take almost anything just to make the pain stop. There's nothing wrong with wanting the pain to stop, it's the type of medicine you choose that may cause horrible repercussions. There is medicine that will numb the source of the pain for a moment in time, then, there is the surgery needed to get to the root and dig it up and destroy it so that true healing can actually take place. For years after my relationship, I chose temporary "maintenance meds" to soothe my emptiness because, honestly, I didn't identify what my problem was. It was like I was taking an antacid for a toothache. I was all wrong. All throughout my life, I seemed to attract men who were unavailable as it were. Those who were married or dating always seemed to be the ones who caught my eye, or whose eye I caught. When I became attracted to them, I didn't always know their situation, but eventually it was revealed.

Not all of my relationships ended up with physical intimacy, but I formed emotional strongholds with these men, which can sometimes be just as destructive. I enjoyed their company, and it didn't matter at the time that I was only able to see them when they were available. The only thing that mattered was that I was getting the attention I needed by way of conversation and/or physical intimacy. Something inside me knew I was once again being used and I was frustrated because they were never single, but they were always willing. For the life of me, I couldn't understand why. So many of you, my sisters, have settled for this type of life just for the sake of having someone in your life. You play the tough role and think that you are in control. But like an addict, you say to yourself, "I can stop this whenever I want." But can you? I remember it like it was yesterday, the day those words were spoken to me that would eventually reveal the presence of a generational stronghold. I was in my mother's kitchen with my sister and I was going on and on about this relationship I was in at the time. To say relationship was a stretch because I was with someone who was not MY boyfriend, but he was involved with someone else.

As I gave the details of my "relationship" and reveling in the excitement of the forbidden, my sister said to me, "oh don't worry about it, all Bynum women are like that." Just like that. Now, imagine if you can, the best slow motion scene from your favorite movie, that's how I felt the day she said those words to me. I saw her lips move and heard the words, but everything around me seemed to be moving in slow motion. Was I supposed to be relieved that I had reduced myself to a level where I was not worthy of an appropriate relationship? Was I supposed to simply settle in for the ride for the rest of my life that said it was the norm to be second and not first and only? Was it OK to settle for sharing a man? Sharing a man? To make matters worse, today's media has placed a stamp of approval on being the side-chick and unfortunately many of my Christian sisters are watching this mess and dismissing it as "entertainment" and "keeping it real" or "having balance". Again, these are my thoughts and feelings. I love y'all, and because this issue is so close to my heart, I live to see you set free.

That day, those few words were branded into my soul and I knew at that moment I didn't want that to be my story. Of course, I didn't know to identify it as a generational stronghold at the time, and I didn't run out of the kitchen saying, "God is going to use me to break this stronghold, honey child!" It was some time later with spiritual revelation and teaching that I was able to identify it as a generational stronghold. And, it was years after that revelation that I finally accepted the fact that God had sovereignly chosen me to break those chains. Whatever the enemy has attached to your family and is now being manifested in you, you don't have to live with it dominating your life. You can break free! I don't care how long you've wrestled with your issue; freedom awaits you and your family. As you are reading this, God may be depositing in your spirit to break the stronghold that has attached itself to you. Yield to His leading and be set free!

The enemy knows that as long as you and I struggle with these strongholds, the longer it will take for us to operate effectively in our assignments in the Kingdom and life, in general. In military terms, a stronghold is a fortress; a fortified place normally used for safety. But these generational strongholds keep you from God's safety. Its walls are so tall, deep and wide that we can hardly see our way out. Now, did I get out of my relationships right away? You see, I didn't get into my lifestyle overnight and I would be naïve to think I would be delivered from it overnight. Not that God couldn't do it overnight, but in order for us to get the lesson, He typically takes us on the scenic route. The problem with not knowing a generational stronghold exists is that we will settle for dysfunction. Our esteem will get so low that bitter things taste sweet. I am so disappointed when I see my beautiful sisters settling for relationships that suck them dry of their self-esteem. They find themselves giving away their precious treasures all for the sake of "love" and waiting and hoping for him to come around and make an honest woman out of them. I lived this way for so long even at the expense of taking the life that grew inside of me for the sake of saving my face and doing away with the shame; now only to be faced with a void in my life that may never be filled and the tearful memories of my selfishness. That is why I have been tasked with this assignment; to help set you free.

But what was I to do? How would I break free from this cycle of destruction? The only thing I knew was that my life had to change. I wish I could sit here and write that I girded up my loins and went straight to the frontline of this battle like a soldier, but that would not be true. Did I understand what this assignment entailed? No, not really. Was I aware that I would be required to change my lifestyle? Yes, indeed. I was not ready for that because what I was getting was so good I couldn't fathom giving that up; even if he did belong to someone else.

In the midst of our situations, we throw away all reason and sensibility. We don't realize that the chains of those strongholds are getting tighter and tighter and before long our lives have been wasted on something or someone that never intended to bring us into our ordained place in God. It hasn't affirmed who we are and it hasn't made us better people. DECREE AND DECLARE RIGHT NOW THAT YOU WILL NOT SETTLE AND YOU WILL BE FREE! After 46 years of life I have yet to experience a beautiful, life-giving relationship with a man. This is partly due to my choices early on in my life when I didn't know my self-worth, and now it is due to the fact that I will not settle for "some" of anything or anyone. I feel compelled to stop here and let you know that it's not easy. Please do not read this and think that I do not struggle. The enemy doesn't give up that easily, but neither do I! God knows exactly how he made me and what moves me. The enemy has studied me, and he knows it, too. Praise God, I've long since stopped being somebody else's "other". My sisters, you may not be the "other", but aren't you tired of being the five or ten-year girlfriend and after you've pushed out one or two of his babies, you've settled for a living arrangement and not true commitment through marriage? You are so much better than that. Break the chains now and receive what you're worth. Before God delivered me, I had always been the "other", never the "one and only". I had always been good enough for the moment or a breath of fresh air while they were in transition from separation or divorce, but never the chosen. As much as this hurts to write, it was my reality and I must share with you to help you avoid the same mistakes.

My behavior mirrored what I had witnessed as a child, but never dreamed it would be my story. I remained bitter for years of my life because for so long I blamed the stronghold in my life and the family tree from which it grew. Breaking free from your stronghold is going to take work, but you can do it. It will not be in your own power, but only by the power of the Holy Ghost. We must yield whole-heartedly to His work in us.

Now that I understood what was as work in my life, I had to agree to do something about it.

GOD'S HAND

Most people go through a good portion of their lives without ever asking God if He has a plan for them to fulfill. They wander through life taking each day as it comes only to lie down, rest and start the cycle again in the morning. They are on a continuous path of the "same old - same old". I, too, had been living this same existence, thinking I had all the time in the world to do whatever I felt grown and bad enough to do. *Psalm 39:4 NIV says: "Show me, Lord, my life's end and the number of my days; let me know how fleeting my life is."* Then came the day I realized that God had His hand on me at a very early age, weaving an intricate tapestry that would become my life. Not that I recognized it at the time but the events that were woven into my life would become the person you and I witness today. You see, the thing about tapestry is it doesn't start out a beautiful work of art, but separate threads that must be put under pressure and woven together to make a delicate masterpiece unique all its own. The threads of my life are many. They have shaped my life in the past which has made me who I am today.

With God's grace, those threads will continue to weave who I am to become in the future. Those threads are colored with great days and accomplishments, but they are also stretched by highs and lows, low self-esteem and abuse. I have made a lot of choices throughout my lifetime, some of which I would have to admit lacked wisdom. But, in the midst of my choices, good and bad, God has somehow caused each of them to work together for my good and His glory. Romans 8:28 (KJV) "And we know that all things work together for good to them that love God, to them who are the called according to his purpose." My life doesn't read as some horrible tragedy, nor has it played out as a fairytale. Somewhere in between I found myself trying to find just where I fit in. Each experience in my life added an extra layer of texture to my divine purpose. Would I have chosen the route God chose for me? Probably not, but His ways are not my ways and His thoughts are not my thoughts. I had to live the life given to me ultimately for you. You thought there was no one who could possibly understand what you are going through. You feel as if you are being punished for some grave mistake from your past. I am here to tell you that is not true. My pain had a purpose, to bring you out and over into your promise land. It is my prayer that my story will connect with something inside of you and provoke you to movement, growth and deliverance. God has His hand on your life. It may not always look like it, but He does, take it from me. When you finish reading this, you will see that God's hand comes disguised in a whole lot of ways – even by way of a generational stronghold.

Growing up middle-class, I guess you could call it, I never knew what it was to struggle. We had a house in Edmondson Village and a house in Harford County at a time when the residents of Jarrettsville weren't trying to see any black faces in their neck of the woods.

Somewhat sheltered as a child, I grew up having everything I could ever want. While I enjoyed being a spoiled child, I didn't know it then, but it worked against me as an adult. My parents didn't struggle to provide for me, and whenever I desired to try something, they made sure it happened. One memory in particular was when I wanted to learn to play the piano. My Daddy bought a baby grand piano and struggled to get that thing down in the basement. I was enrolled in *The Peobody Conservatory of Music* and took lessons. When I didn't want to practice, I didn't. So when the time came for me to go to class, I was chastised by my instructor for not practicing my lesson. I began to cry and after class told my Daddy I didn't want to go back. He didn't make me go back, either. I often think on this memory because I wonder where I would've been today had I continued through the hard stuff, the challenges of which make us strong. So, I said all of that to say, parents, stop giving your children EVERYTHING so easily, you're only hurting them. But, nevertheless, I was a Daddy's girl until the day he died, and I remain one until this day, in spirit. My father had only a sixth grade education and managed to become an entrepreneur and owned seven record stores throughout Baltimore City, and while most of my friends were going to Kings Dominion or hanging around the house on weekends, I was working. I'm grateful for that experience because it has made me appreciate the value of work and the satisfaction of being an entrepreneur myself. When I started to reflect on where God has brought me, it became evident to me several years ago that God's hand was on my life even at the tender age of three weeks old. God already knew the assignment He had chosen for me and that I would need a spiritual foundation on which to stand. He provided that foundation for me through my babysitter who I later adopted as my god-mother. As a child growing up, I would spend large amounts of time with my godmother. She introduced me to who God was. I have fond memories of her in the mornings at 6 am laying prostrate before the Lord. And, if you were in her house at that time of morning, you were laying prostrate, too. I didn't appreciate it back then, but now I see that those seeds planted have grown and the fruit has nourished me through the years.

I've always been a creative soul wanting to sing and write. I can remember putting on puppet shows in my back yard for a nickel and people actually paid to see them. I made my puppets from those large tin cans fruit and vegetables came in. Now why didn't anyone tell me I could've gotten infected with those raggedy edges? I actually did get nicked a couple times, hilarious! I was always famous in my mind and I guess somewhere deep inside I always knew I would be in a place where others would know me, too. But on the journey to my dreams, I would have to encounter some detours. My detours came by way of generational strongholds.

Each of us has a divine date with our purpose and as wonderful as that sounds, we do not get there without a journey and yes, sometimes not without a fight. As I've come to discover, the tougher the fight, the greater the destiny and purpose. Unfortunately, we are not granted a prescreening of what our lives will become nor the twists and turns we will have to encounter to get to that divine place ordained for us by God. We are not privy to the bumps along the way that will sometimes leave scars that last a lifetime. For if we did know, we would take another route, I know I would. We are simply given an invitation to this thing called life and how you and I show up to the party will determine our experience and outcome.

Realizing how God had His hand on my life didn't happen overnight. You see, when someone says that God's hand is on their lives, they are usually alluding to the blessings and overflow manifested on a day to day basis. While all of that may be true, please do not miss the presence of God's hand in the not so pleasant experiences in your life, either. God's hand is not only meant to be a providing hand, but a guiding hand through the ebb and flow of this life. I have lived long enough to know that sometimes God's hand doesn't look like God's hand. Moreover, if we are not careful, we will miss his hand. I know, because I almost missed it. Let me not fake the funk, there were a few times that I did miss his hand. So don't feel like since you've missed some of God's messages and promptings that all is lost. God's grace will afford us another opportunity to get it right. I was in my mid to late twenties before I acknowledged His hand upon my life. It wasn't until I had to travel some very rough terrain that I realized something else was going on. I lived a pretty normal life, gaining all of the normal things that any normal person would at that time in my life. Nothing spectacular to mention, I was just going about life, until one day I came to the realization that I had to identify and face something that subtly controlled me and had no intention of letting go. In order for me to be successful I would need God's help to be set free and remain free.

No one ever wants to believe that God could be the

maestro of some of the pain that we must endure. I know I didn't want to believe or accept it. I always felt as if I was being punished for the bad decisions I've made, because certainly none of my circumstances could come from a loving Father molding my life into something beautiful. Or, so I thought. Perhaps you've had those feelings because of some less than shining moments in your life. I'm here to tell you that those moments, if you are willing, can be the very things that God uses to bring you into your appointed time; your expected end.

MY SCARLET LETTER

The enemy knows what gets to me
What makes me want to run and hide
The enemy knows what pierces my heart
And causes the tears to flow like a river
The enemy knows what hurts me to the point
where I just concede, it's that Scarlet Letter that just
continues to bleed

Taking the blame for someone else's sin
Taking the fall for someone else's lust
Collecting all of the scorn from other people's lips
Wearing it as my garment, it seems a perfect fit
Branded to me was this letter I don't deny its
place in my past
But how can I erase the stain or will this
imprint forever last?

Deliverance has come to me but somehow I reject it
Believing in some small way that I was unworthy of it
Telling myself that I'd done something again, this time
Whispers that drown out all reason
Stares that awaken my sleeping ghosts
Will my scarlet letter ever be erased?
Giving me a chance to plead my case?
I have a choice to make
Do I run or do I stay?
Running gives my accusers satisfaction
While staying silences their tongues
I'll need courage to choose this one

We've all played a part in someone else's hurt
My portion has been bought and paid for
When you remember all of my indiscretions
You forget the scarlet letter you wore

"Come now, let us reason together, saith the Lord: though your sins be as scarlet, they shall be as white as snow; though they be red like crimson, they shall be as wool." Isaiah 1:18 KJV

Perhaps you are familiar with Nathanial Hawthorne's The Scarlet Letter, an 1850 romantic work of a woman who conceived a child as a result of an adulterous affair, yet tries to gain redemption and dignity by starting a new life. Everyone has a scarlet letter of sorts, not necessarily the result of an adulterous affair, but one that people have attached to you in remembrance of your past or some indiscretion. People want to make sure that you never forget the time in your life when an appetite became so overwhelming that it caused you to make decisions with long lasting repercussions. They seem to forget that their stomach has growled on more than one occasion. Dr. Charles F. Stanley has a quote that reminds me beautifully of the principle of sowing and reaping. He says, "We reap what we sow, more than we sow, later than we sow." We witness this principle so clearly in the natural, but it is true in the spirit.

I realize that some of the behavior in which I engaged is still bearing fruit, and if you happen to be one of the few who do not have a past, this book isn't for you. I had a period of time in my life when I wore a scarlet letter. And it was through my generational stronghold that this scarlet letter made its debut in my life. But, through the grace of God, repentance and forgiveness, He has erased every trace, stain and broken the chain that once was attached to me.

When we are born, the first relationship we experience is that of our parents. We bond and learn how to get a response to our every need all from the relationship with our parents. Growing up, for all I knew, my parents were as normal as any other mother and father. As my parents, they provided everything that I needed and I wanted for nothing, ever. I didn't know enough to think it strange that my father was only at the house a couple times a week. I don't even remember ever asking why. What I do remember is watching my mother and seeing how she handled her man. Unknown to me at the time I was learning how I would one day relate to men and how they would treat me.

Mommy was what you would call a "good woman". Beautiful and petite, I can easily see why daddy fell for her. I watched her and learned how to validate and affirm a man. You drew his bathwater, cooked his food, and took good care of him and he would take good care of you. As an adult, I look back at this set up as one of obligation - Daddy took care of us and provided a lifestyle of comfort while he also took care of his other family and that made it okay. I could hardly wait to be able to do those things my mom did for my man one day because I saw the "benefits". Unfortunately, I also learned from my father what I would accept from the men in my life. With my mother accepting sub-par treatment, on some rare occasions I was afraid for her when I saw my father's temper flare and he'd put his hands on her. When she didn't leave, I felt it must be something that came with the territory because everything always went back to normal and we were a happy family again. So, many years later when my man would put his hands on me, neither did I leave, I would tell myself to stop making him angry.

With this age of social media, I have read so many stories of my precious sisters being abused and even killed by the men in their lives. You may be reading this book right now knowing full well that this is your current situation. People on the outside looking in can easily make the comment that you shouldn't take that type of abuse. That would be true. However, when your self-esteem is so damaged, like mine was, you take the blame for everything...and I mean everything. You always reason within yourself that things will be better tomorrow, or accept the cheesy attempt at apology made by your abuser.

But take heart, there is freedom and new life that awaits you, my sister. God is waiting to take you by your hand and lead you out of your situation into everything He's created for you. You will never see it if you are blinded by dysfunction and you don't feel you're worthy of it. I'm here to tell you that you are worthy of it and God wants to make sure you have it. God's hand is on your life and don't you forget it!

THE STRONGHOLD OF LOW SELF-ESTEEM

Fast forward years later when it was time for me to experience my first relationship my tools were sharpened and ready for use. Indulge me as I revisit a previous chapter for a moment. I met my first boyfriend in Junior High School at age fourteen and we stayed together off and on until I was twenty-six. He was my high school sweetheart and I was in love. At age fifteen I experienced every "first" with him. I remember my first kiss after gym class one day. He just rolled up on me and planted one on me. I just stood there afterwards like a dear in the headlights thinking, "umm, he'd done this before."

I remember my first sexual encounter with him and walking up that long hill home afterwards thinking "wow, I can't believe I just had sex! I'm a woman, now." I put into practice what I'd learned much earlier in life; the lesson that seemed to say put your man first no matter what. As our relationship progressed and we graduated, I made the mistake of being more interested in him, but never being interested in me. I believed he cared for me, even loved me, but just wasn't the one for me. No matter how we tried to make it fit, no amount of my "good woman" ways was enough to keep him true to me. In some ways this was a flashback to my parents' relationship. Pouring everything I had into my relationship, I demanded nothing in return, but to keep me by his side. He was my world; he was everything to me. Everyone else around me saw that I was giving more than I was receiving and tried to steer me in the other direction, but I wasn't having it. I was needy and insecure. I needed to show him that I could be faithful just like I'd learned from my mother. That's what would make a man stay, or so I thought.

This generational stronghold found a toe hole and made its way into my life and would not be discovered until many years later. I would experience some of the same mishandlings as my mother had and not even think it to be strange. My life was on a course destined to repeat and unfold just as my parents' lives unfolded.

There is an enemy of our souls who seeks to steal, kill and destroy. This same enemy causes low self-esteem which distorts our view and causes us to accept less than what we deserve. While in this relationship, I found myself behaving in ways that I am almost ashamed to write about within these pages. My insecurities had me doing foolish things such as driving across town at 2 am to someone else's house only to find his car there. I sank to one of my lowest moments when after listening to his voice mail, I discovered he was meeting someone later. I had my girlfriend drive me half way down Rt. 301 and I hid in the passenger side floor of her car trying to catch him. We almost got busted because he saw her and walked over to her car to speak. It's a funny story, now, yet shameful that I felt compelled to sink so low for a man. You see, this reckless behavior will have you dragging innocent bystanders into your mess. Yes, I checked his pager along with some other nonsense before I got wind of how fearful and wonderfully made I was. One night at my apartment he woke up in a panic asking, "whose bed am I in?" I know you're reading this and saying, "this chick should have gotten the message by now!" You would be absolutely correct. I

43

should have gotten the message…I did not. The stronghold. After years of being mishandled, friends and pastor praying with me, I finally came to the conclusion that enough was enough and let go. Look, who am I kidding? Better said is God snatched me away from it. Wait! Before you start cheering me on, know that I left broken and scarred emotionally and little did I know I would begin a journey of searching for love in all the wrong ways. With self-esteem damaged (well, there really wasn't much to work with, anyway) I sought to relieve my pain and regroup the best way I knew how...another relationship. If he didn't want me, surely somebody else would. This time, it wouldn't matter that he wasn't "mine", just so long as I had him when I wanted him. My last relationship had taught me that with all of my attempts to be faithful, that didn't get me anything but pain, so I released the notion of having to have a man all to myself.

When I think of the cycle of those who came in and out of my life, I am reminded just how mistaken I was to think I could gain comfort and relief from my pain by engaging in temporary escapades. It becomes so easy to fall for an illusion of happiness when you never experienced the authentic. I was a passenger on the emotional rollercoaster over and over again, with its ascents to the top, only to be dropped at record speed because I was never "the one". Why was I never the one? I had learned to be a good woman from my mother and I longed to demonstrate that to a good man. Somehow that good man always eluded me and I gave my treasure away recklessly.

As fallout from my past relationship, I was dealing with deep hurt and rejection. Subsequently, I found myself repeating the same behavior that manifested itself in my mother's life and which hurt me in the first place. I eventually became attracted to a young man who was engaged to someone else. My scruples were out the window by now and all I could see was him in my view. I would stop at nothing to take this ride. Still unsure of my worth, I thought this relationship would give me the validation I so longed for after the relationship I had just left after so many years. After several months of my own bliss like you can't even imagine, conviction came over me and I came clean. It didn't go quite as I had planned, but there I was the star of a monumental mess. I didn't know how to handle this one. In my past relationship he made it look so easy, although he never confessed! I witnessed the pain and hurt left in the wake of my confession. Look, I was new at this so I never stopped to think about how I felt the many times I found out I was being cheated on. I was like a bull in a china shop. I just needed to prove to myself that I still had it going on, even if my boyfriend didn't want me. But it was this incident that branded me for what seemed like a lifetime. Once more and more people found out, I became the one with the scarlet letter. Granted, it was my own fault, but damn! Yes, I was a marked woman, so to speak. Women would see me and hold on to their husbands or significant others just a little tighter. I got the hairy-eye from insecure wives and girlfriends on the regular. Little did they know, I didn't want anything they had; not in the least...TRUST ME! I saw what I wanted, and believe me, I knew how to get it. The thing about the scarlet letter is that you even get accused of things you didn't do. I am the first to come clean and say that I've tasted forbidden fruit a time or two in my past, but from that one incident in particular, I was blamed on multiple occasions for improprieties; none of which were true. Yes, folk stopped speaking to me as if I was a one woman show. Last time I checked, it took two to tango.

During this period in my life, I thought nothing of my behavior. I was hurting and this new found form of relief medicated my pain. No amount of intervention was going to help me. My girlfriends tried to help me but my feelings overrode my sense. I became someone I didn't recognize. My soul was searching and crying for love and affirmation just as I had given in the past. I didn't set out to conquer any guy that caught my eye, I was making a genuine attempt to find the one that would recognize and claim the jewel that was me. In my naiveté I never realized that the affirmation had to come from me and me alone. What I needed was to understand that my true worth and identity could only come from knowing myself and the God who created me. I didn't know how He felt about me. Let's face it, God is a man, could I even trust him? I didn't know how I was supposed to feel about myself. My behavior was out of character. I had never been that type of girl. When we as women are not taught what it means to love ourselves and what we should and should not accept, we act out in ways that compromise our true selves. We become someone else in the mirror of deception.

When desperate for love, we settle for what looks and feels like relationship. Those momentary encounters will come and satiate us then leave us until the next time. But this is all a charade if you don't know your worth and value and what you bring to the table. I was fully aware of what I brought to the table, but my emptiness was so great, that I stuffed my God-sized hole with physical debris that I confused with love.

I was well aware of my inappropriate behavior; my journals tell the story of my remorse and deep longing to break free. I'd write to the only one who understood me...the pages of my explicit journals. I cried out for deliverance, and year after year after year those pages were filled with the same cycle and pleas for help. Little did I know that the difficulty to break free was all due to the stronghold getting stronger.

Truth be told, I still feel the judgmental stares years later from my false accusers. But their stares don't move me now because God has since forgiven and restored me. He has restored me to the place of being able to minister to other women. And God will restore you, too, if you allow Him to do the work in you.

THE SPIRIT OF A THING

My pastor taught me that the spirit of a thing is stronger than the manifestation. The strongholds I faced throughout my life began as a spiritual attack generations before me. They began to gradually manifest themselves in my life through the spirit of low self-esteem, sexual sin and my relationships. Years after my first relationship ended, we managed to see each other on occasion. It was like a pull that in my mind I knew was destructive, but I just couldn't seem to let go. The bible says if we drive out one spirit and fail to replace that vacancy with something else, the evil spirit will come back seven times stronger. (Matthew 12:43-45). Although I was praying for deliverance, my prayers were few and far between because I was not sure if I even wanted to be free. Most of my prayers were to put us back together and not "thy will be done." Once again, the spirit of low self-esteem will have you craving even the bitter things. This spirit was so strong that it seemed to only attract men that were in relationship with someone else or married. That was how this stronghold gained its genesis and perpetuated itself down the line. Time after time I struggled to break free from my bondage of fornication and couldn't figure out why I wasn't being successful. I would try with all of my might not to place myself in compromising situations that would force me to make a choice. Let's face it if I had to make a choice, the choice was always going to be to satisfy my flesh.

Underestimating the strength of a spirit can lead you to destruction. I vacillated back and forth for years. This stronghold was so tight that I was actually visited by spirits on a few occasions. The spirit of fornication and sexual sin would manifest at times late at night as I slept. I would be pinned to my bed and I could feel a tongue going up and down my neck and in and out of my mouth. A couple of times, I awakened to have my legs in the air. Ok, I see, y'all aren't ready for raw. This book isn't meant to be a cute little tale of how to get free, but I am here to pull the covers off of the enemy and tell you how he will come to you. Spiritual warfare is not to be entered into lightly. I don't go looking to engage in it, but if you have a prayer life, you're engaging in spiritual warfare. If you don't know what you're dealing with, don't play with spirits.

First and foremost, you must acknowledge the stronghold. As long as you deny or refuse to acknowledge it, it has its grips on you. Low self-esteem, rejection, pain and anger you name it, I felt it. I was born into this world, the product of the love between a man and a woman, but the enemy had plans to ruin my life.

Oftentimes I felt as if I was living a double life. Wearing the mask in front of others while secretly fighting against this stronghold that had me behaving like a dope fiend. One minute saying I was free, the next minute calling my pusher for my next hit.

SOLITAIRE

"Let's play solitaire" the Lord said to me one day
I have a mighty work for you, so at this current level you
just can't stay
I know a private place where there's no noise from the crowd
Those secret thoughts and visions you can speak to me out
loud
This place is exclusive so some things I'll insist you leave
behind
Making sure there are no distractions; the only voice you'll
need is Mine
Others may come to try and rescue you from your state
I have so much more to offer you if all you'd do is wait
So enjoy the view, pick any spot that's right for you
Your stay can be a blessing according to the attitude you
choose
You're special to me- I had to bring you here to see
Those tests that looked like mountains were all for your
testimony
"Let's play solitaire" the Lord gave me the rules to begin
Thank you for solitaire because in the end I win

During my process of deliverance God had me in a place of isolation. Being the one chosen to break this stronghold, I could not continue to operate as usual. Not only did this stronghold manifest as sexual impurity, but along with it came other spirits that God needed to purge from me. God had plans for my life and they would not come to fruition while this thing had me in a choke hold. When God has an assignment, sometimes He must remove us from all of the noise and distractions in order that we can hear and see clearly. When we are struggling with issues that take our focus from Him, God will do whatever is necessary to get our attention. Sometimes that comes in the form of isolation from people and things. Other times God will allow events and circumstances to come that will force us to turn to Him and listen attentively. In my case, the next attention-getter was my Lupus diagnosis. Initially, it felt as if I was being punished for everything I had allowed to attach to me. I had no friends in which to confide about this stronghold and everywhere I turned seemed like a closed door. In this season of my life, I learned to pray and listen.

Initially, my prayers were self-centered and I just wanted some relief from the disease and the loneliness. But, this time was ordained by God to get me to see me, as I really was – broken, insecure, rejected. I would never have imagined that I was all of those things, yet my behavior clearly said otherwise. You see, a trait of this stronghold was vanity and since I'd been rejected by my so-called relationships, I needed something to validate me and make me feel wanted and accepted. I relied on my looks. I was real easy on the eyes and I had a body to match. I knew this and the attention I received from others would surely manifest confirmation. Modesty was not in my vocabulary and I was proud of what I had accomplished by working out and taking care of myself. When the Lupus diagnosis came, I was devastated. "How could this happen to me?" I took care of myself, was in the gym religiously and this is the thanks I get? Was I thinking about how it would affect my life? No. I was worried about how it would affect my appearance. As a matter of fact, I didn't start to see my doctors on a regular basis until the disease started changing the way that I looked. As a result of the disease, I had to deal with all of my hair falling out and growing back differently. Over the past 7 years, "Lupie", as I affectionately call her, has manifested all over my skin. It's left severe scarring that is said to be permanent. It has indeed challenged my esteem. This is just another way God has used to reinforce his creative design in me. I am not my skin, I am fearfully and wonderfully made!

All of a sudden, not only did I have to continue my fight of staying free, now I had this disease that was trying to take over my body. Deliverance is something like going through withdrawal. I had days and nights when all I wanted was to make that phone call, but God was there to get me through my shakes until I could see the light of day. At other times, I blatantly ignored His help.

Sometimes troubles in our lives come to get us to move and other times it is to get us to a point where the only person we have left to turn is the Lord. A solitary place is a good place to hear from God. The noise from the outside world is brought down to a minimum. A solitary place may be the loss of a job, the loss of a home, the loss of a loved one or even the loss of health. A solitary place is any place that leaves you feeling alone and seeing no other relief in sight.

While getting settled in my solitary place, it seemed at first that God was punishing me. Again, I felt that God was punishing me for the relationships I had allowed myself to get into. The enemy wanted me to have this type of mindset so I would have a defeated mentality. When I continued to pray the Lord sent people in my life with a word of correction and a word of encouragement. That's what the word does; it cuts and heals at the same time. I had an opportunity to get a deeper understanding of the Old Testament during this time. The Old Testament is an illustration of the overwhelming love God has for his people. All of us, like the children of Israel, are guilty of sin. We, just like them, were on a cycle of sin, crying out for God to help and once He sends us the help we're right back in sin shortly thereafter. The good news about the Old Testament is that even though God chastised the children of Israel for their sins and disobedience, He always sent a word of healing and restoration to demonstrate his constant, unconditional love for them. Once they repented, that is.

I began to move to my solitary place in the middle of 1998. In the midst of asking God for direction and trying to hear from him, some other things were distracting me. In May of 1998, I met a gentleman and we hit it off right away. He was everything I usually wanted in a man. Boy, the enemy took his time getting this package together. He gave this man the right height, weight, complexion, hair, looks and personality. What this man did not have was Jesus. He was not saved. The only thing saved was the change in his pocket after he broke a dollar. I know, I know, that should have put up a red flag. But the package was wrapped so beautifully; I had to rip it open. What blinded me was the fact that he was single and I took it as fair game.

As I began to see this gentleman, I saw things in me that were not pleasing to God. When I was with this man, I was not trying to witness to him. When I was with him I honestly forgot I knew the Lord Jesus. Whenever I brought up church, he would cringe and protest that there was a time and place for that type of talk. Sometimes I truly thought God would have to come from glory and smite me in the head with a brick to make me see the signs this man was so blatantly giving me all along. These are definitely times to start thanking God for his mercy.

Our faith will be put to the test. How many of us know that it is impossible to hear from the Lord let alone listen and follow directions when we have carnal distractions on every hand? I found out the hard way. Have you figured out yet that I always have to take the scenic route in learning lessons? The more I told the Lord and myself that I was going to live a holy life, the more I saw this man. I held out and held out. The more I saw this man, the weaker I became. Until one day I slept with him and even had the nerve to get up, go home so I could get dressed for church. The more I slept with him, the more I became vexed. The louder my spirit screamed to be free from this fornication, the longer I stayed and the more comfortable I became in my solitary place. Things began to fall apart in my life. Not once did I stop acknowledging the Lord. I sincerely hungered for the Lord with all my heart and a closer walk with Him. I just was not willing to be totally sold out to everything. I fasted, prayed, I anointed myself, my bed, my house, you name it...EVERYWHERE. But what good is all of that anointing if I'm not right?

All at once it seemed I began to lose things I depended on. Sometimes we do not think that one thing has anything to do with the other when they are so different. Romans 8:28 "and we know that all things work together for the good to them that love God and are the called according to His purpose." I moved back home with my parents and my comfort level was stripped. It was not business as usual as it was when I had my own place. But that too soon changed. It would take more than a change of residence to change my mindset.

This solitary place became very uncomfortable. I had to adjust to living with other people and their habits. I had to be mindful of my attitude during this process because eventually I began to entertain friends at my parents' home. It was unrealistic to even think that no one would visit me where I lived. The key to making productive use of your solitary place is what you do while you are there. If we become content, we will fall deeper into the rut we are trying to get up from. We must use our time wisely. In the solitary place, we must wait (attend to; as a waiter) on God while we are waiting (in anticipation; readiness) on Him. I had to continue to bless the Lord and be grateful for the provisions he had continued to make for me. No matter what the test, sister, we must make a conscious effort to bless the Lord at all times. The enemy wants us to turn our backs on God and forfeit our blessings and our promise. There is a connection in the spirit to everything that happens in the flesh. There are consequences to pay for our disobedience. I continued to lose people. By the end of 1998, the Lord had removed every person from my life that stole from me, my spirit. Sisters, continue to believe that the Lord orders our steps. All of the good, all of the bad, they all are ordered. The plan of the Lord will be revealed in time. It is our responsibility to get the mindset to obey the Lord no matter what the cost.

The more I prayed and listened, the more God uncovered who I was and who I was to become. I saw who was for me and who was against me. If you find yourself in a solitary place, do your best to be prayerful and discover what God may be trying to say to you. I won't tell you that staying in that place is easy or desirable, for that matter. I am simply asking you to embrace all that God has to offer you while the two of you are communing alone. You will eventually see that it was time well spent in order to break your chains, however long the season.

THE WORK CONTINUES
It Grabs You

Just when you think you've overcome this thing, something happens to awaken your stronghold. It pulls you like a magnet to a piece of metal. You do your best to break free, but not only are your emotions and spirit attached, in most cases; your soul is tied to that stronghold. A call, text, or maybe even a thought can awaken your stronghold. A drink or one lottery ticket can cause you to slip and before you know it, you are back where you've worked so hard to be free from. I know all too well. There were times when I would go months without falling and I felt as if I'd accomplished something. But as soon as the right trigger was pulled, I found myself entangled again with the yoke of bondage that had threatened to keep me locked up for my entire life. I found myself in a cycle of falling and praying and falling and praying.

Once I'd get to a point where I felt as if I was strong, I would let my guard down and ease up on prayer and accountability, and that was always when the enemy would get in an attack. I would lead myself into a false sense of security thinking I could make that phone call and not be affected. When I felt lonely is when I was most susceptible to my stronghold and the only comfort I could find was in God's arms. You are not alone. Being delivered is an ongoing process, which requires work.

When have you ever known anything worth fighting for to be easy? Becoming a successful business owner isn't easy; it takes work. Becoming the best at your craft doesn't happen overnight; it takes work. And surely protecting your future and the future of generations still alive and coming after you is worth fighting for…that will take work. Taking a passive stance against that which is trying to keep you in a dysfunctional position is unwise, to say the least. Again, you don't have to be a believer to be a victim of a stronghold, these bondages do not discriminate against race, religion, gender or ethnicity. It is an equal opportunity nuisance. For you to dismiss what has been holding you or your family members hostage is generational suicide. Whether your method of healing comes through therapy or the One who is the Healer of all things, the Lord Jesus Christ, you must decide you want to get healed.

How does that process look for you? Perhaps it will mean removing yourself from everything toxic in your life: people, things or even activities. This may sound foolish, but for a long time I couldn't even shop in Victoria's Secret because of the feelings that store aroused in me. I'm telling you, God knows how he made me…and it is good. I just had to learn to harness all of that "goodness" until the proper time. You see, it's the deception of the enemy that will have us believe that something as silly as shopping in a store couldn't possibly ignite a small ember that will continue to burn until it becomes an inferno. At that point, it's too late. It's the little foxes, that spoil the vine.

As you seek to break free, stay committed to the work and the journey. Find yourself an accountability partner that will call you on the carpet, and one you can be brutally honest with. Honesty is a central ingredient in your recipe to deliverance. Do the work, see yourself in the future and declare that you're well worth the fight.

HE PROMISED TO KEEP ME

"He's a keeper" that's what the church mother said
"Keep your mind on Jesus, baby,
He'll give you the rest you seek"
There's not much difference between us you see
I speak out loud the thoughts you keep in private
Somehow the blame is always placed on me
My past haunts me; my future beacons me
Into a place where only the anointing can cleanse
Realizing I'm not the only one wrestling with private sins
My essence, my spice dreams to be awakened by your
touch
But sanctification is the call I must answer for my
virtue is worth far too much
So when thoughts of my man arouse me to the brink
of no return
By your Spirit Lord, please take control
Don't trust my flesh or my mind, oh will I ever learn
He promised to keep me
If my mind is stayed on Him
He promised to keep me
To my sensual desires don't give in
When visions of you keep me like a rose with morning's
dew
When evening comes and desire won't seem to leave
Somewhere inside I'll remember…
He Promised to Keep Me

I'M BRINGING YOU WITH ME

As I write, I realize that God has been ever so faithful to me throughout my journey. His kindness and mercy are much better than life to me. This journey may have taken longer than it needed to take, but ultimately it has brought me to my appointed time and place within the Kingdom. For so very long, I vacillated back and forth on whether or not I would even accept this assignment for fear of the accountability that would surely be required upon rendering a "yes" to God. Ultimately, the satisfaction in knowing God saw fit to use me to play a part in your freedom and the grace He continues to lavish upon me is so worth the journey.

My divine assignment to aid in the destruction and annihilation of generational strongholds, however they may manifest, brings fear and trepidation because at the end of the day, I am still only human with shortcomings just like you. This is why I am sure that through the work of the Holy Ghost, I can do all things through Christ who strengthens me.

This book was not only to tell my story, but also to allow you to see and possibly identify whatever has been holding you back from your destiny in God. This book is to also bring my family members, and all who read this book into a place of unshackled living and ultimate freedom.

It is God's desire to see you free from the bondage of addiction, strongholds and attitudes that have hindered your growth for so many years.

In order to come on this journey, you must be willing to

do the work. Understand that there will be days, weeks, months or even years factored into your date with deliverance, but I am confident in you, through the Lord Jesus Christ, that you can make it and come out on the other side as a victor.

Be sure to stay in God's face through prayer and daily bible reading, for these give us access to God's strategic plans for our situation.

I want you to be aware that you do not come through generational strongholds easily, it is a process of discovery, acknowledgement and action to which you must be committed. Strongholds should not be taken lightly; you should care whether or not one has been attached to you and your family. I do not want to see you waste another year struggling with chains of bondage when you can be free to live out your God-given assignment. Stop trying to dismiss those little frustrations that you've been dealing with for far too long. Don't allow anyone to speak things into or over your life that attach any type of negativity to you or those attached to you. There is life and death in the power of the tongue, so be mindful of what you speak and what you receive, as well.

My sisters, I am taking you with me as I walk out this divine assignment to see you live a life of freedom. What would this journey be if I had to go on it alone? I need you there to encourage me as I encourage you. Ultimately, you will encourage someone else to take the journey once you witness just how liberated you become. It has been my pleasure to open a chapter of my life to you and allow you to see the secret places of which I was once too ashamed to claim ownership.

The treasure which God created, which takes the form of what you now see, has been tried and proven and is no longer defiled. I am ready to be used for God's plan and purpose.

For what the enemy meant as evil, God has used it for my good…and yours. Amen.

ABOUT THE AUTHOR

Stayce L. Bynum, native and resident
of Baltimore, Maryland, is a licensed
minister, poet, entrepreneur and
author with a unique and creative
soul which houses a sincere passion
for addressing the issues of women.
Her life has been touched by many
of the same issues that affect women
today, and she is determined to use
her gifts as tools to help them
become free.

No stranger to the bondage of low self-esteem and
generational strongholds, she understands the destructive
tendencies and behaviors that compromise one's destiny in
God. Upon understanding and accepting her assignment,
Stayce began to release her pain through her poetry and in
2004, birthed Sista'Worth Greetings, a greeting card line for
the empowerment of women. Since that time, she has
increased her card line to over 80 titles to help break the
chains of generational strongholds and low self-esteem
among the daughters of God.

Stayce has also become a living testimony of the healing
power of God. In 2000, she was diagnosed with Lupus SLE
and has since used her journey to minister to others with this
disease. To facilitate this endeavor, through her Facebook
group, Stayce hosts a weekly vlog titled *Sistas Living with
Lupus*, which educates and empowers women of color living

with Lupus.

Stayce's life experiences and creativity have been the fuel for her projects and allows her to use her own unique voice while ministering to other women. Stayce has survived through the fight of living with generational strongholds, and the struggle of breaking free. She has the battle scars to prove her victory over illness and is determined to see someone else come through victoriously. Stayce is a writer and has written for online Christian publications, printed magazines and The Baltimore Examiner as Christian Singles Examiner. She holds a Bachelors degree in Management from The College of Notre Dame of Maryland.